I0793648

Video Games

LEVEL O

DECODABLES BY jump!

Teaching Tips

Lilac Level 0

This book focuses on teaching the earliest readers how to read a book by following images and text from left to right.

Before Reading

- Discuss the title. Ask readers what they think the book will be about.

Read the Book

- Encourage readers to describe what they see on each page.
- Ask questions to help readers understand the story and its progression.
  - What happens at the beginning of the book?
  - What happens at the end of the book?
  - How do we know?

After Reading

- Ask readers what part of the book they liked best. Have them find the page or pages that showed this.
- Have readers imagine a different ending for the book. What else could have happened?

5357 Penn Avenue South
Minneapolis, MN 55419
www.jumplibrary.com

Decodables by Jump! are published by Jump! Library.

Library of Congress Cataloging-in-Publication Data is available at www.loc.gov or upon request from the publisher.

ISBN: 979-8-88996-759-0 (hardcover)
ISBN: 979-8-88996-760-6 (paperback)
ISBN: 979-8-88996-761-3 (ebook)

Photo Credits
Images are courtesy of Shutterstock.com. With thanks to Getty Images, Thinkstock Photo and iStockphoto. Cover – carballo. p4–5– Lukassek, Michael Pettigrew. 6–7– wavebreakmedia, XiXinXing. 8–9– wavebreakmedia. 10–11– AboutLife, Africa Studio, p12 – gorillaimages.

About Reading

When we read a book, we go from left to right, like this:

Some books just have pictures, like this:

Some books have words and pictures, like this:

AC 644 KS

NEW GAME
CONTINUE
OPTION

GAME OVER

PLAY AGAIN?

YES NO

Close the book and flip it over to read
Team Games!

Close the book and flip it over to read Video Games!

About Reading

When we read a book, we go from left to right, like this:

Some books just have pictures, like this:

Some books have words and pictures, like this:

Teaching Tips

Lilac Level 0

This book focuses on teaching the earliest readers how to read a book by following images and text from left to right.

Before Reading

- Discuss the title. Ask readers what they think the book will be about.

Read the Book

- Encourage readers to describe what they see on each page.
- Ask questions to help readers understand the story and its progression.
    - What happens at the beginning of the book?
    - What happens at the end of the book?
    - How do we know?

After Reading

- Ask readers what part of the book they liked best. Have them find the page or pages that showed this.
- Have readers imagine a different ending for the book. What else could have happened?

This edition is published by arrangement with Booklife Publishing.

North American adaptations © 2024 Jump!
5357 Penn Avenue South
Minneapolis, MN 55419
www.jumplibrary.com

Decodables by Jump! are published by Jump! Library.

Library of Congress Cataloging-in-Publication Data is available at www.loc.gov or upon request from the publisher.

ISBN: 979-8-88996-759-0 (hardcover)
ISBN: 979-8-88996-760-6 (paperback)
ISBN: 979-8-88996-761-3 (ebook)

Photo Credits
Images are courtesy of Shutterstock.com. With thanks to SuperStock, Getty Images, Thinkstock Photo and iStockphoto. Cover– Daju Project. p4–5– TY Lim, Peathegee Inc/Blend Images. p6–7– wavebreakmedia, XiXinXing. p8–9– wavebreakmedia. p10–11– AboutLife, gorillaimages.

Team Games

LEVEL 0

DECODABLES BY jump!